Relaxing
color by
numbers

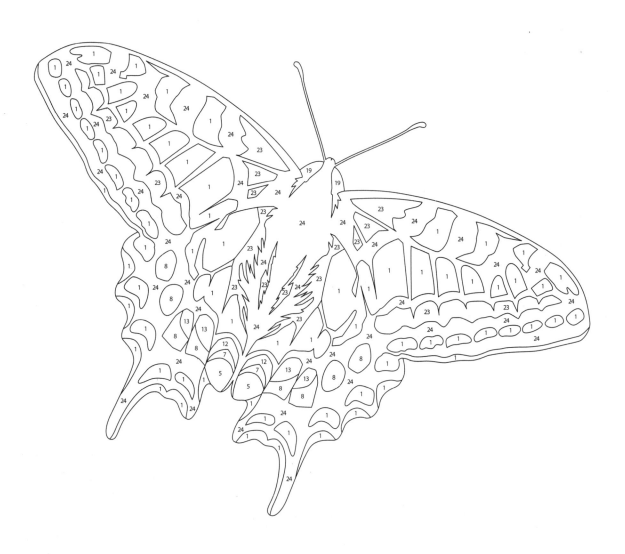

Relaxing
color by numbers
numbers

David Woodroffe

SIRIUS

SIRIUS

This edition published in 2020 by Sirius Publishing, a division of
Arcturus Publishing Limited,
26/27 Bickels Yard, 151–153 Bermondsey Street,
London SE1 3HA

ISBN: 978-1-83940-949-3
CH004924NT

Printed in China

INTRODUCTION

Discover your love of coloring and focus your mind with this fantastic collection of color-by-number images. Each image is numbered so that, by following the color key on the back cover, you can make the subject come to life and create an artwork to be proud of. Try to match each of the colored pencils in your set with a color from the key—you can even label your pencils with a number to make things easier. It is a process that requires concentration, time, and care, especially when filling in the smallest color areas. Try not to rush through it—the process of coloring itself can be hugely rewarding and relaxing.

The images are inspired by nature, art, music, and meditation, as well as patterns and optical tricks. All are designed to engage you, concentrate your mind, and make you aware of the rich diversity of the world around you.

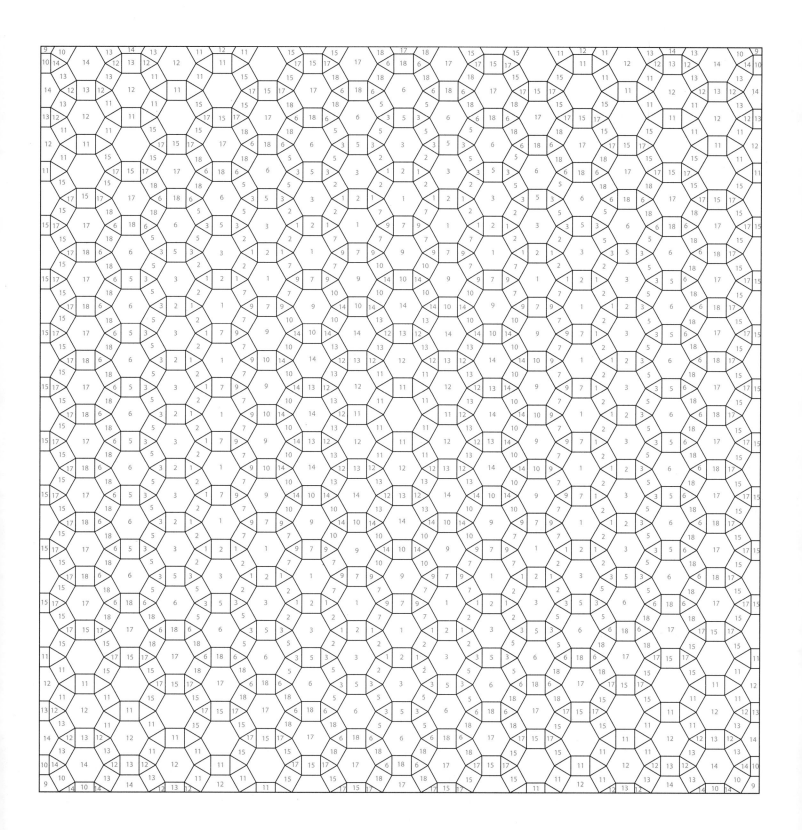

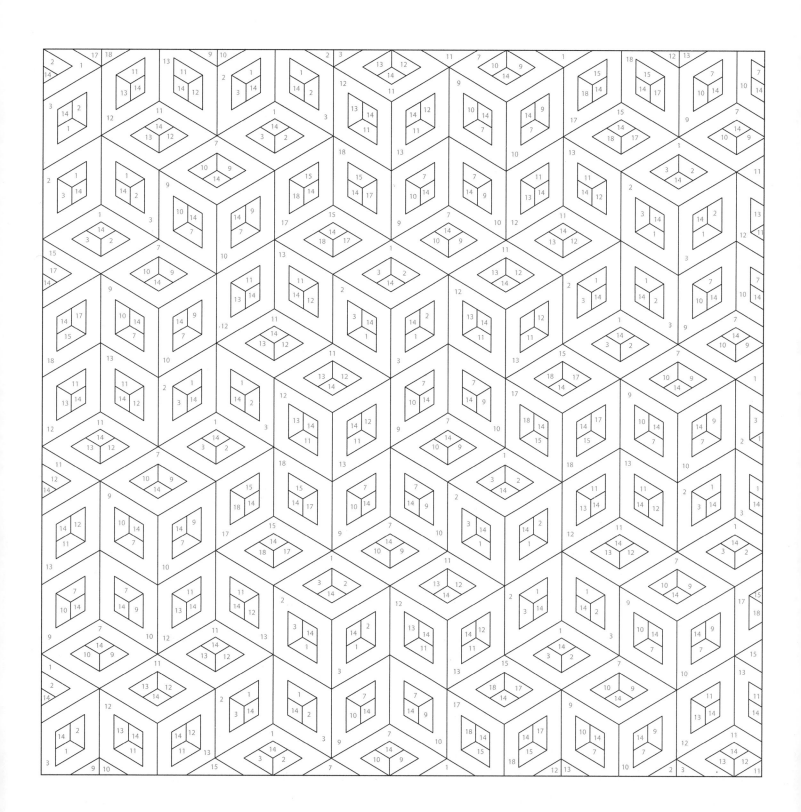

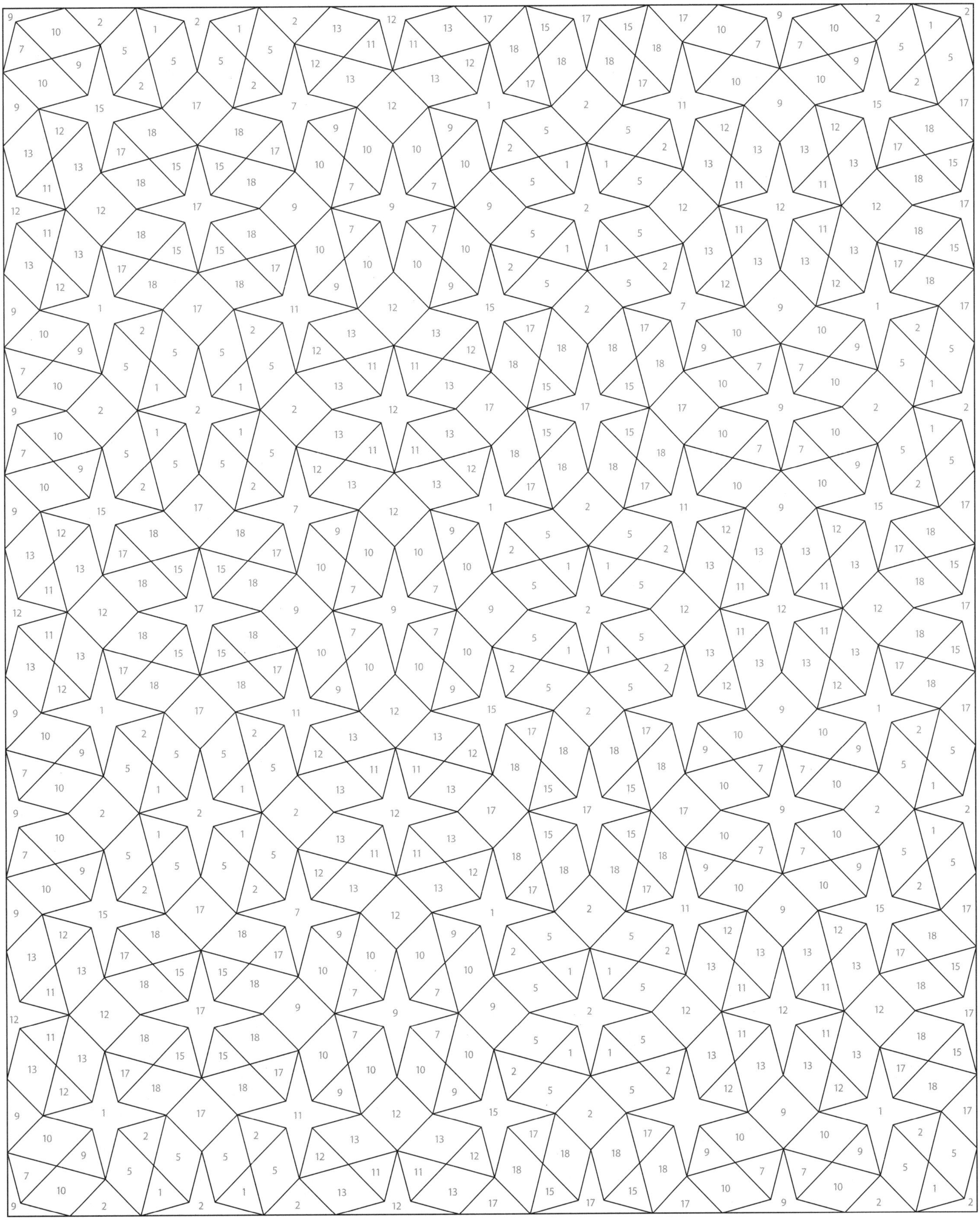

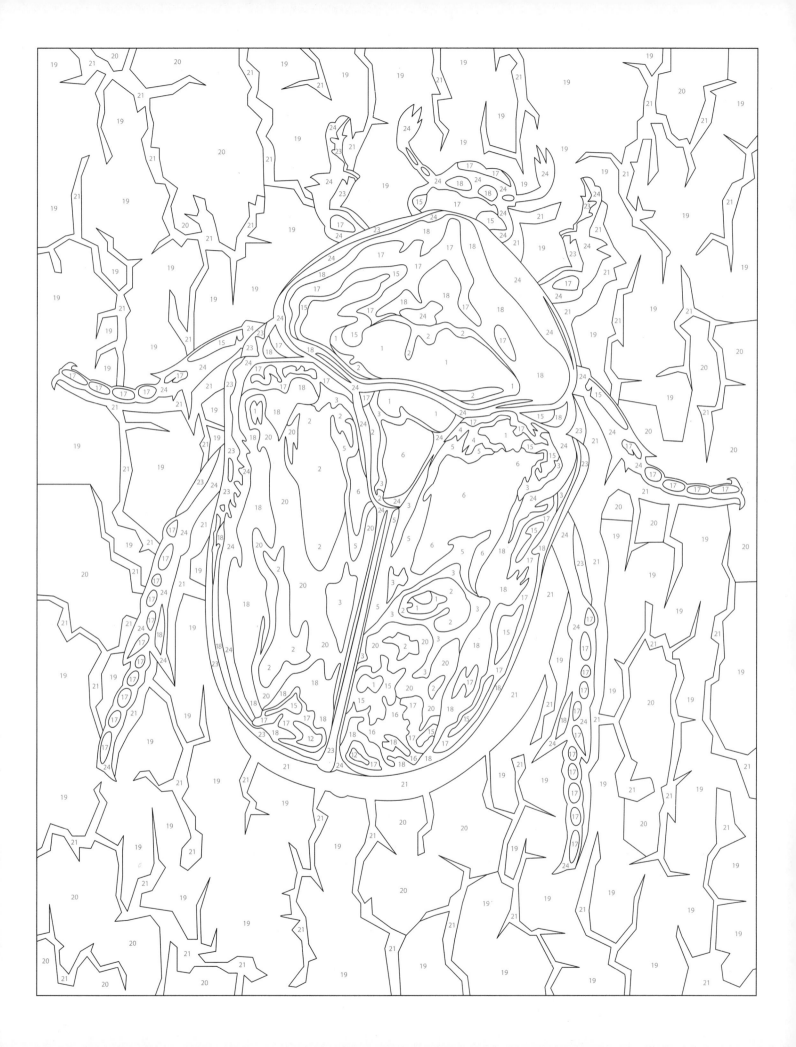

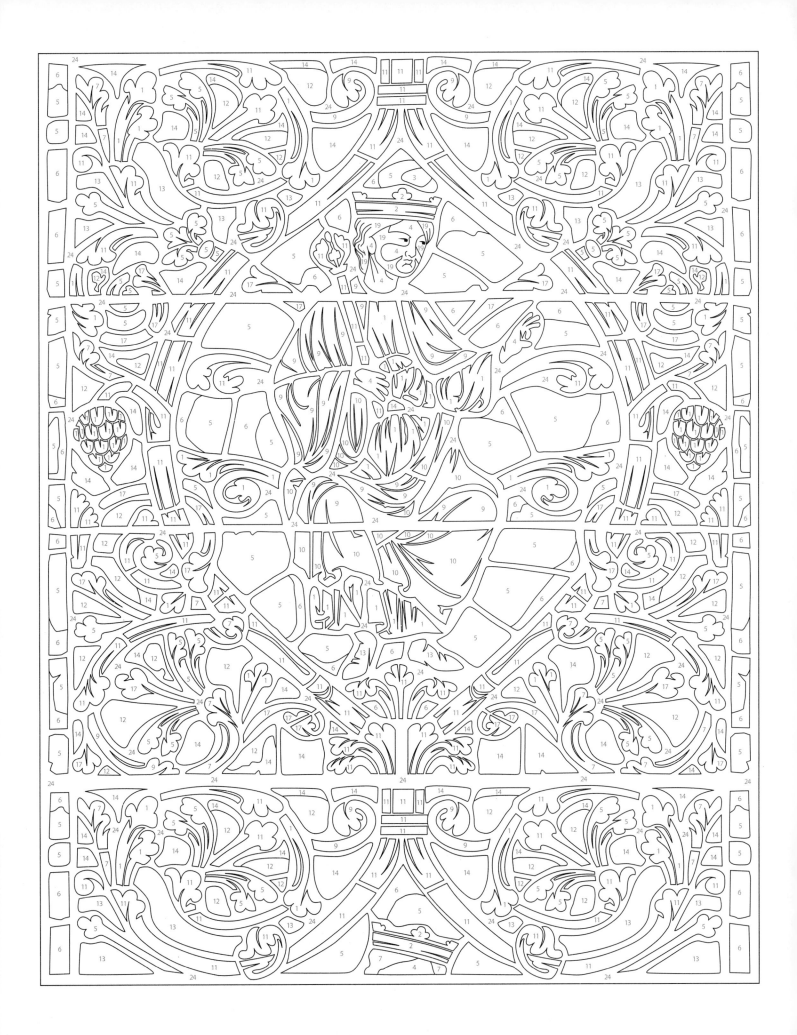

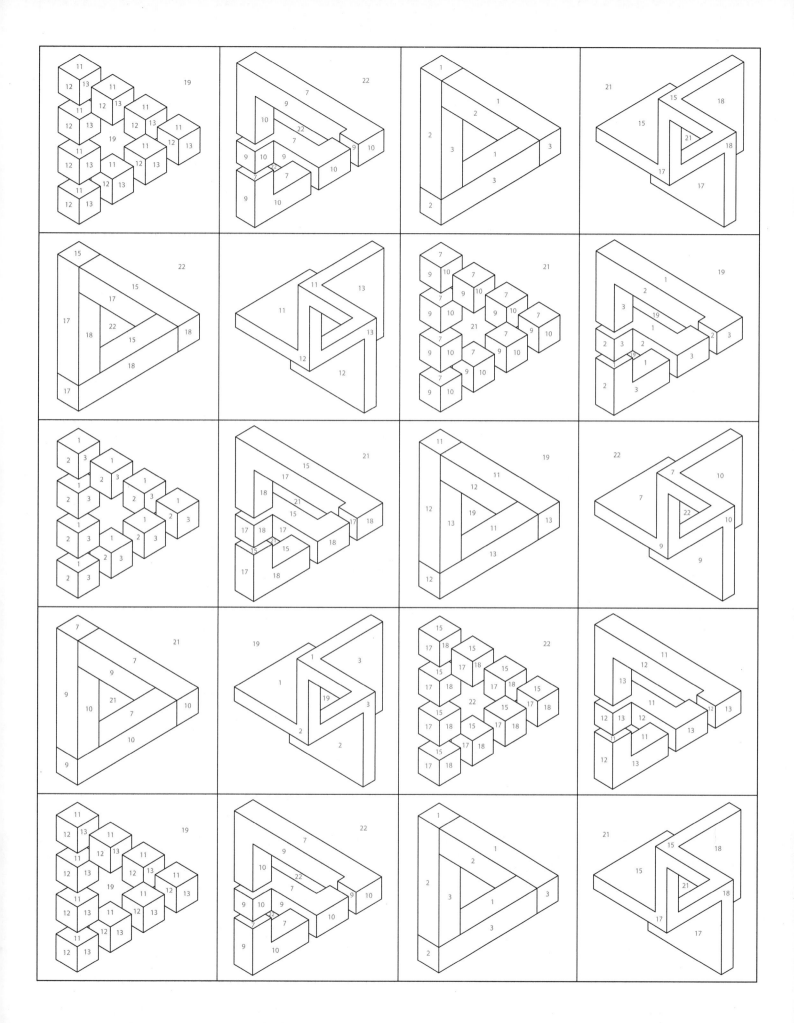

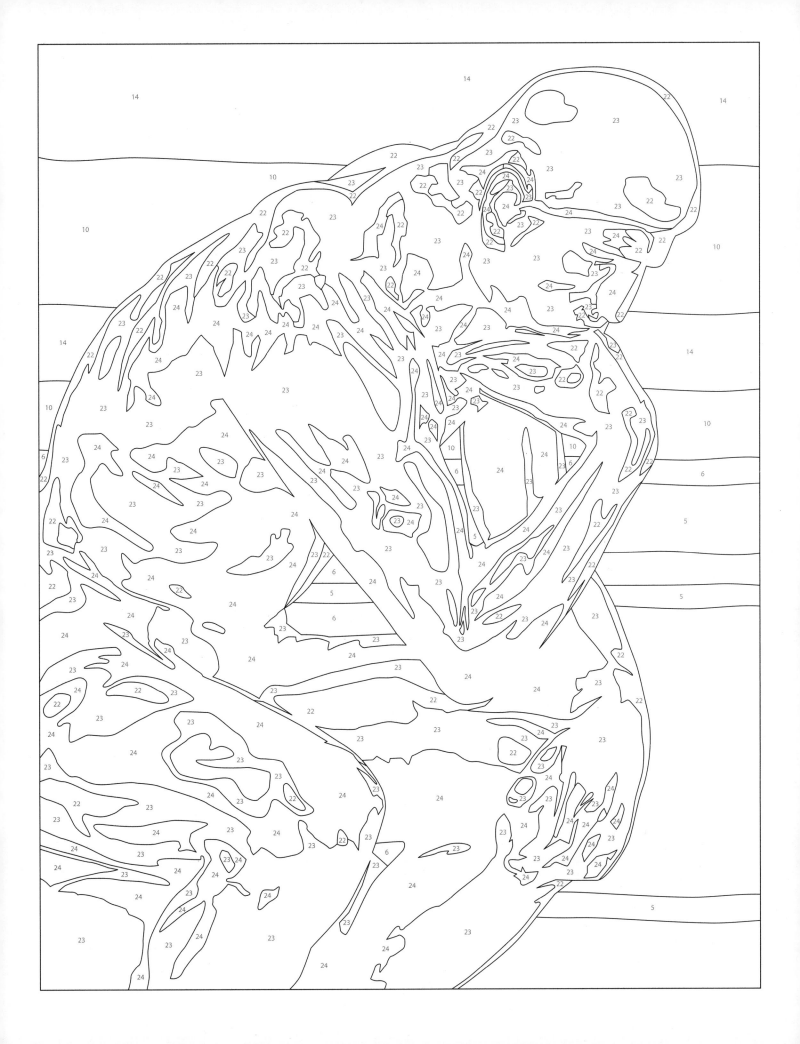